Praise for

There is NO TIME

"This book may be 'brief' but its message has BIG implications for missions – especially those focused on church planting. For compelling reasons cited by Dr. Nyquist throughout his parable, Short-Cycle Church Planting teams should now be the norm amidst the uncertainties in which missions is conducted today. The rapid, yet culturally sensitive method to … get there … get busy … then get out, is especially applicable to church planting in urban/ suburban populations. And that is where most people in the world are living today. That is why this book is so timely and relevant to those engaged in completing the task." – MARVIN J. NEWELL, D. MISS., Executive Director, Cross Global Link

"The ideas contained in *There is NO TIME* are not just clever theory. Paul Nyquist has done serious time in the trenches and knows what is effective in ministry. As a church, we have invested ourselves significantly in the principles of this book because they work. Our hearts resonate with the urgency of the mission and the team-based approach as the biblical way to do ministry. Anyone who wants to light a fire of passion in the local church around missions and church planting needs to read this book carefully." – BRYAN CLARK, Senior Pastor, Lincoln Berean Church in Lincoln, Neb.

"*There is NO TIME* is a quick but compelling read. It offers a way of doing church planting that forces the entrenched traditional methods to make room. We can all agree that our hope does not rest in plans but in Christ. Yet every once in a while, a plan centered on Christ excites the mind and soul for the hope to come; this work does just that. This book is a must read for any church or organization that is serious about finding the best ways to plant churches among people who do not have the gospel." – JEREMY PACE, Director of Missions & Church Planting, The Village Church in Highland Village, Texas

"*There is NO TIME* is a quick and easy read, but the image left on the thoughtful reader will penetrate and remain. The Short-Cycle church plant is not intended as a 'one-size-fits-all' model, only an intelligent attempt to shorten the time needed to plant indigenous churches in appropriate settings. This is an important contribution to the ongoing dialogue to be more creative and strategic in our mission. Highly recommended!" – JEFF ADAMS, PH.D., Senior Pastor, Kansas City Baptist Temple in Kansas City, Mo.

"*There is NO TIME* highlights that missions in today's fast paced world needs to change. Assumptions and methods from my days as a missionary are not adequate for today's world. Short-Cycle Church Planting is a valuable methodology already being used and bearing fruit. As a former missionary

and mission administrator, and now as a professor of missions, I highly recommend a careful perusal of this small volume that I believe will revolutionize missions in the 21st Century." – FRED H. SMITH, PH.D., Director, School of World Missions, Professor of Cross Cultural Studies in Toccoa Falls College, GA

"Dr. Nyquist has put several important, relevant, biblically-based mission insights into what turns out to be a page-turner. The story format is being rediscovered as a means of conveying truth effectively...it works well in this case. You won't be disappointed. Read and be prepared for a paradigm shift that transforms your thinking concerning mission in today's uncertain and rapidly changing world." – RICHARD M. BIERY, M.D., President, Broadbaker Group

"Paul Nyquist provides a creative overview of Avant Ministries' new 'Short-Cycle Church Planting strategy' in his missionary fable, *There is NO TIME*. I like the way he weaves out-of-the-box thinking into this imaginary strategy session in the mountains between old college friends. I wonder how much of this story is really fiction! *There is NO TIME* should serve well as a training tool on the basics of this fast and focused church planting strategy. By the way, I couldn't put the fable down until I'd finished! Can't wait for the sequel." – MIKE BARNETT, PH.D., Elmer V. Thompson Professor of Missionary Church Planting, Columbia International University

"You talk about packing a wallop! Wow! This captivating, easy-to-read fable will cause believers everywhere to experience a paradigm shift that uncovers a fresh, exciting, sensible, and most importantly, biblical approach to missions in the 21st century. Brace for impact!" – MARK TROTTER, Northwest Bible Church, Teaching Pastor in Hilliard, OH

There is
NO TIME

There is NO TIME

A Missionary Fable

J. PAUL NYQUIST

To Cheryl,

your love for me

   for life

   and for our Savior

continues to humble me
I consider myself blessed

TABLE OF CONTENTS

ACKNOWLEDGEMENTS

Unlike many, I have had no abiding desire to be an author. However, I do have a red-hot passion for global evangelization. This book emerges from the milieu of that passion.

The concepts that serve as the framework for this story did not originate with me. Instead, they have been discovered and honed by the collaborative creative synergy of an incredible Executive Team with whom I serve at Avant Ministries. Thank you men, for the privilege of standing in the foxhole with you: Scott Harris, David Rathbun, Scott Holbrook, Dean Callison and Grant Morrison.

Thank you to Brian Herzog and his crackerjack communications team. Your legwork, problem-solving and project management made this book a reality.

Thank you to Lynda Morrison, Sandy Klaus and Natalie Nyquist who worked editorial magic on a limp manuscript. I appreciate your diligence and servant hearts.

Thank you to the initial "guinea pigs" of Short-Cycle Church Planting®—the Avant team in Poland: Kenn and Doreen Oke, Kirk and Dannel Blackwell, Tim and Spring

Becker, Ruth Estella Dauber, Cathleen Schwab, and Janell Frey. You took the risk of investing part of your lives in an unproven model and saw God's power accomplish amazing things. I will be forever grateful for your faith, vision and courage.

And thank you to the Lord Jesus Christ, who is building His church around the world.

After this I looked and there before me was a great multitude that no one could count, from every nation, tribe, people and language, standing before the throne and in front of the Lamb. They were wearing white robes and were holding palm branches in their hands. And they cried out in a loud voice: "Salvation belongs to our God, who sits on the throne, and to the Lamb."

REVELATION 7:9-10

INTRODUCTION

The world has changed. Missions has not.

Before the turn of the twentieth century, when many mission agencies were birthed by the Student Volunteer Movement of the 1880s, including Avant Ministries, travel was by steamship; communication was difficult; and terms were long. Even fifty years ago, when the conclusion of World War II brought a tidal wave of new missionaries, little had changed.

But now warp-speed change fueled by globalization and terrorism has gripped this world. The static has been replaced by the fluid. Old paradigms based upon assumptions and not realities prove to be increasingly ineffective.

Today communication is instantaneous and global. Today travel is fast and relatively cheap. Today the doors to countries open and close quickly as governments form, fall and form again. Today the most unreached nations are also the most unstable. Today there are more unbelievers alive than at any other time in history. Tomorrow there will be even more.

What does this mean for the evangelical missionary enterprise? It means that present and future effectiveness requires a willingness to look at new models, new structures and new paradigms.

The model presented on the pages of this book is not intended to be viewed as the only way the pieces of the puzzle can be reassembled. I am not that presumptuous. However, it does represent one plausible attempt to address the problem. It is a model that draws equally from academic research, field experience and the corporate world. And it is a model that has rapidly accumulating evidence for its effectiveness.

I have been heavily influenced by learned men who have sought to communicate conceptual truth not in a didactic fashion but via the medium of story. The fable that follows represents my attempt to communicate in the same manner.

I

A DATE WITH DEATH

His captor looked like a mere child. Perhaps thirteen years of age, certainly no more than fourteen: a body still in prepubescence. But despite his youthful age, he showed a hardened edge. His eyes were steely black and riveting. His posture was stiffly erect and alert. His hands fondled the weapon of choice for the rebel armies: an AK-47.

The makeshift jail was a crumbling mud hut with a sparse thatched roof deep in the bush. Dave had been dragged here three days ago by a small but heavily armed force. They kidnapped him from his modest home on the missionary compound in Sitaki, along with one other missionary comrade and three Westerners abducted from nearby parts of the city. The purpose of the capture was purely financial. To these rebel minds, Westerners always possess riches. Repeatedly in the hours since his abduction, harsh demands were made for money.

How he longed to satisfy their greed and perhaps gain

3

THERE IS NO TIME

his escape! But he couldn't. For security reasons, Dave had learned as a missionary to carry very little cash. The rebel leader, a foul man lacking both patience and a conscience, did not believe him. After one last demand, laden with curses and threats, the leader, called Bontu by the others, angrily passed sentence on Dave. He had become weary of the game. Dave would be executed by firing squad at sundown.

As the minutes ticked away toward his impending execution, Dave fought to keep his composure.

"Lord, is this it? Is this Your will for me? Mere target practice for a bunch of trigger-happy thugs?"

He had no question this rag-tag band would litter his body with lead when given the chance. He had seen their ruthless, even joyful destruction of monkeys and parrots since his capture. Evil was not a strong enough word for them.

"But why me? And why now?"

Dave had only been in the West African country of Tognumou for six years, pioneering a church plant among the Fonu tribe. While the country had enjoyed a reasonable measure of political stability, at least according to West African standards, the society began to implode last fall. The government, led by a strong-man military dictator, reneged on promised water rights to the farmers in the arid south. As livestock began to die and crops began to fail, the farmer-peasants grew restless and vocal. The Fonu, who were primarily in the north, were not directly affected. Fishermen by trade, their skills were visible in the water, not on the soil.

But most of the country was profoundly agitated. Therefore, in order to show their displeasure with the government's new water policies, farmers set up a series of blockades in the capital city of Dabala. The protests seemed to grow in number by the day—peaceable, yet problematic. The government turned a deaf ear to the burgeoning crowds. A stalemate ensued.

And then came the unforgettable and the unforgivable. The dictator, who tired quickly of these burdensome blockades, eschewed any further diplomacy and recklessly ordered the military to do whatever was necessary to regain order in the city. With a blank check in their pocket, the military leaders chose to send a powerful, albeit bloody, message. At midnight, Russian-built tanks rolled into streets, followed by several regiments of crack troops. Without waiting for any signs of submission, the massacre started. Gunfire and mortar shells rained through the night. At daybreak, the gory results were visible for all to see. Hundreds of protesters lay dead in the streets. Blood-spattered buildings everywhere. Predictably, the government claimed victory on all its regulated radio stations.

At first, the nation was in shock. But then, from nearly every quadrant of the country came rumblings of revolt. Farmers turned in their plowshares for automatic weapons and rocket-propelled grenades. Revolutionaries found willing allies among radical leaders in North Africa. Before three weeks had passed, the country was mired in full-scale civil war.

As a missionary among the peaceable Fonu people, Dave, like his colleagues, sought to dismiss any threat of personal danger. The hard-core fighting was far away from their rural location. While a team member regularly monitored the situation and kept in constant contact with the U.S. Embassy, no one had a clear assessment of the grassroots infiltration that was happening—until the rebels broke through the security fence of the mission compound and took Dave and another missionary captive.

The drama of the past seventy-two hours had now led to this: a date with death. With no Bible to read and no friends to support him, Dave felt increasingly alone. He squatted against the wall, put his head in his hands, and nervously prayed.

The child-guard paid him little heed. The sun would set in less than an hour.

2

OUT OF AFRICA

Gunfire suddenly erupted, sounding like a long string of firecrackers. Rebel soldiers, who had been relaxing in hammocks in the heat of the afternoon, scrambled to their feet and began screaming instructions at each other. A few shot wildly with their automatic weapons at an enemy they could not yet identify. The chaos quickly intensified, with the sound of footsteps running in all directions. The bullets kept flying, whistling through the canopy of trees.

Dave instinctively flopped face-down on the ground against the wall of the hut, covering his head with his hands. The sound of AK-47s filled the air, punctuated by an occasional mortar shell. One rebel leader, who had a crazed, frantic look in his eyes, thrust his head into Dave's prison hut and jerked the boy-guard out into the battle. Dave thought momentarily of attempting to escape, but immediately realized the futility of such a plan.

Instead, he feverishly prayed. Again.

~~~

It ended almost as quickly as it began. The silence was deafening. No more gunfire. No yells. No screams. Only the muffled sound of voices, speaking in firm, measured tones. Dave cautiously peeked through the doorway of the hut, peering into the battle-induced haze. He saw several bodies of rebel soldiers strewn across the opening in the settlement, their hands still gripping their automatic weapons. He inched through the door, still crouching low, unsure of what had just transpired.

Leaving his death-shed, he crawled along in the dusky shadows listening for the voices. Were they friends or foes? Should he flee or should he see who had ambushed the rebel camp? Dave's mind, weary from the trauma, didn't immediately produce an answer. He froze, just steps outside his hut, hidden partially by the trunk of a mango tree.

Suddenly the cold steel of a gun barrel pressed against his left temple.

"Don't shoot," Dave cried, throwing his hands in the air.

"An American." Dave heard the soldier say in the Fonu language. The gun dropped, but Dave kept his hands high in the air while still kneeling on the ground. Out of the haze, a military officer appeared, walking toward him. Dave could tell from the many bright medals hanging on his chest he was a high-ranking officer—probably a general.

"What your name?" the officer asked in broken English.

"David. David Peterson." Dave replied in English. He dropped his hands to his sides and hesitantly stood to his feet.

"What you doing here?" the officer demanded.

"I am a Christian missionary with All-World Missions. I live in Sitaki but was abducted by these rebels three days ago. They kept asking me for money. I didn't have any—at least not as much as they wanted. So they planned to shoot me."

The officer studied Dave, listening intently to his words. For a moment, Dave wondered if his life was still in jeopardy. Then a small smile creased the officer's face.

"You fortunate man, Mr. Peterson. All other hostages killed. Some by rebels. Some in crossfire."

Dave gasped audibly when he heard those words. He turned his head away from the officer, struggling for composure. He felt tears well up in his eyes. One of those killed had been his missionary comrade.

"Can you help me?" he asked through his tears.

"Yes," the officer said. "We escort you to safety. But you must leave country soon. You no go back to Sitaki. Too dangerous. We take you to American Embassy and they take you home."

There was a strange ring to the word *home* for Dave. Tognumou had been his home for six years. He had become accustomed to it. But the home that the officer spoke of was America. Like it or not, Dave was returning to the U.S.

After what he had experienced in the past 72 hours, Dave was more than ready to go.

3

HARD QUESTIONS

Counselors have a name for it. It is post-traumatic stress disorder. Soldiers who have been in combat often suffer from it. So do children who have been exposed to extreme trauma, such as rape, violent attacks or abuse. Symptoms include nightmares, flashbacks, sleep abnormalities, depression and a hypersensitivity to triggering phenomenon.

Upon his return to the States, Dave went through a lengthy debrief with mission leaders and an extended series of sessions with a counselor who had special training in post-traumatic stress disorder. At the end of the sequence, the consensus was that, by God's grace, Dave had been spared serious emotional scarring from his experiences. What he needed was some additional physical recuperation time. So, he booked a flight to Peoria, Illinois to spend some time with his parents.

Bill and Doris Peterson understood the demands of

missionary life very well. For thirty-five years they had served as missionaries in Venezuela. Dave had grown up in Caracas, watching his father preach, disciple and plant churches. He had fond memories of those days. Churches seemed to get started almost effortlessly. It was a rewarding, fruitful time.

When the Petersons retired from active missionary service four years ago, they relocated to Peoria in order to be near extended family. Dave had been in their home before but never for more than a couple weeks. This would be much longer than that. He was looking forward to it. After all, for a single young man of thirty years of age, nothing tasted better than Mom's cooking!

After just six days in his parents' home, Dave felt rejuvenated. His lingering fatigue disappeared. The occasional nightmare from his abduction in Sitaki ceased. Energy began to pulse through his veins again.

However, one issue continued to haunt him. With his premature exit from among the Fonu people, no church had been established. Dave anticipated living in Tognumou his entire life: learning the language, building relationships, and planting a church. His timeline did not include a forced, early departure from the country due to political strife. His exit left not a developing church but only a few isolated believers who understood and experienced very little about being "church." With West Africa's poor track record for resolving armed conflicts, Dave knew he would not be returning to Tognumou any time soon. Perhaps never.

One afternoon, while reflecting on his aborted ministry, Dave took a long walk in a nearby park. He sank down on a weather-beaten bench overlooking the quiet lake and took a long sip on his vanilla latte. Watching two boys fish from the shore, Dave once again pondered the elusive questions.

How can anyone expect to plant a church when the world is so volatile? Missionaries of his parents' age usually assumed they would stay on a field for their entire career. His folks did. The peace and stability of their field allowed for longevity and productivity. But such political tranquility was becoming rare today—especially in the most unreached parts of the world. Areas most needing the Gospel are also the regions experiencing the most turmoil and conflict. In that sense, Tognumou was not an exception. It was typical. Too typical.

But if you can no longer assume a lengthy ministry in a country, how can you expect to plant a church? This thought challenged all of Dave's missiological training. His teachers and mentors had all echoed the same message: it takes *time* to establish a mature church. You cannot rush the process. It takes time to learn the language and culture. It takes time to build relationships with the people. It takes time to develop leaders. It takes time to establish a self-governing, self-supporting and self-propagating church. It takes a long time.

But the traditional models and training did not fit the realities of cross-cultural ministry in Dave's world. In Dave's world, you had no time. In Dave's world, you could not assume a lengthy ministry. In Dave's world, if a church was to be established, it had to be established faster than in the past. Dave was not content to leave another group like he left the Fonu. The next time, when given the same time frame, he wanted to leave behind a mature church if he were forced to leave.

THERE IS NO TIME

But how?

Dave took another sip of his latte. He noticed that one of the boys had caught a small bluegill. The youngsters peered down at the fish, still hooked and flopping on the ground and jabbered excitedly of their success.

That's what he wanted. He wanted the joy and fulfillment of successful ministry. Not the emptiness of leaving a work hardly started.

But could a church be planted faster? Is it even possible?

Dave slurped the last gulp out of his cup and tossed it in a wired waste container. He knew he was asking the right questions. Now he had to find the answers.

4

TRACKING THE APOSTLE PAUL

In Bible college, Dave briefly studied the missionary journeys of the Apostle Paul—it was a required assignment in his introductory missions class. But now that Dave was asking fundamental questions about church planting, especially questions of a feasible time frame, he knew a reexamination of Paul's ministry was necessary.

Well trained in inductive Bible study, Dave took his Bible, a notebook and pen to a quiet back room in the local library. He opened the text to Acts 13 and started reading, making observations as he went. He charted the cities visited and noted the details of each ministry. Across Cyprus. Then to Perga. North to Antioch and then east to Iconium, Lystra and Derbe. As he marked his map showing the return route of Paul and Barnabas, Dave noticed a fact that previously escaped him. He noticed Paul appointed elders in each of the churches of the four cities he had visited (Acts 14:23).

Paul appointed "elders"? Elders were a clear sign of a

mature church. Dave sat there staring at the text, stunned by the implications.

Certainly this doesn't refer to elders as we know them today, he thought. That would be impossible! The time frame was too short! Suddenly he realized the absurdity of his conclusion. For the one appointing the elders was the Apostle Paul, whom God used to list the qualifications for elders in I Timothy and Titus. If anyone would know whether a person was qualified to be an elder, it would be Paul!

Dave's mind kept racing. *How long did this take? How long did Paul minister in each of these cities?* He dug into some of his dad's reference books he had stashed in his well-worn backpack. The most realistic chronologies had Paul ministering in Antioch for three months, Iconium for five months and in Lystra and Derbe for four months. With the return visit to each city, the total time invested by Paul in these four churches was no more than fifteen months before he appointed elders.

Now Dave's heart was beating faster and sweat formed on his brow. Surely, there is a logical explanation for this. Perhaps the converts were all Jews who already possessed a rich understanding of the Old Testament Scriptures. But the text did not allow for that. While some Jews believed, the indication was that most of the converts were Gentiles from a pagan background.

The facts from historical record were inescapable. *A team of two missionaries planted four churches complete with elders in four different cities, some of which were quite hostile to the message, in a span of only fifteen months.* In future travels, Paul would revisit the churches to encourage them, but it was obvious that after this first journey, Paul felt his work in these cities was accomplished.

Dave let that truth sink into his soul. How had he not seen this before?

With feverish anticipation, Dave paged ahead in Acts to track Paul's second and third journeys. New territory was covered. First Macedonia, then Achaia. But the pattern was similar. Only three months in Philippi and Thessalonica. Just one month in Berea. A longer stay in Corinth: a year and a half. The third journey brought nearly three years in Ephesus, which was the longest Paul stayed in any one location. But even that was less than the normal first term of a modern missionary.

Dave made observations and took notes for nearly three hours. At the end, he sat back in his chair and tried to summarize what he had found. He knew he could not uncritically transfer first century truth into his world. Paul was an apostle. He was not. And, while Paul did have to cross some minor cultural barriers, he did not, in most cases, have to learn a new language in order to communicate to people.

Yet, the conclusion was clear: God is able to establish churches quickly. He did so in the first century. According to Dave's chronology, in a period of just ten years, Paul successfully planted churches throughout the four provinces of the Roman Empire and spoke as if his work there were done. Church planting does not need to take decades.

This left Dave to ponder his dilemma: *Why wouldn't God want to establish churches quickly today? Why wouldn't He want to see the Gospel spread rapidly and churches emerge swiftly? Had His power diminished? Was His sovereignty compromised? Did He love people less?*

Dave knew God had not changed. He left the library

determined to find ways to see God move powerfully and swiftly to establish His church around the world. But he knew he would need help.

5

THE GANG

They called themselves "the gang." Not exactly a creative title, but fitting nonetheless.

The gang was a brotherhood of four buddies who met at Lofdahl College, a small Christian liberal arts school in the Midwest. Although they arrived on campus from different backgrounds, and with diverse interests, early in their freshman year they connected and became almost inseparable. Each successive school year brought a litany of new adventures. They shared rooms, vacations, classes, sorrows and even holidays with each other. They pretty much "did life" together.

Thus, graduation day was bittersweet. The four friends, who had enjoyed life jointly in college, would now travel solo as God led them in different directions. Dave still remembered the tears he wiped away that day as he said goodbye to his beloved comrades. While he had briefly seen a couple of them in the intervening years, the foursome had not been all together since Commencement Day.

Now Dave knew it was time to reunite the gang. He needed them. He needed their encouragement. He needed their input. He needed their sharp minds.

Landis Martin was the most gifted leader of the group. Tall and dark, with rugged good looks, Landis followed in his father's footsteps, receiving an MBA from an elite business school in the south. Two stops later, Landis was now serving as the Chief Operating Officer for a growing biotechnology firm in the Dallas area. He married Haley, his college sweetheart, while in grad school and God blessed their marriage with two beautiful daughters.

Landis had a brilliant mind and was well read. He was a diligent student of both the Bible and the *Harvard Business Review*. Although he could intimidate others with his intellectual prowess, Landis also knew how to have fun. Dave laughed to himself when he remembered some of the practical jokes Landis pulled on people. Sharp, funny, yet not full of himself. He struck a rare balance between pursuing excellence and staying humble. Not surprisingly, Landis was using his leadership gifts in the local church as a member of the elder board.

Ken O'Malley was the preacher of the group. Red-haired and immensely likeable, Ken fell in love with theology while at Lofdahl. Believing God wanted him to serve in local church ministry, he went to seminary after graduation. There Ken flourished not only in the classroom but also in practical ministry. Gifted in his ability to learn languages, Ken excelled as a teacher and preacher of the Bible.

His first ministry was as the Education Pastor of a large church in Tulsa. Now he served in a pulpit ministry as Senior Pastor of a medium-sized community church in

Illinois. Married with three children who all inherited his red hair, Ken had an infectious laugh that could light up a room. Most people, including Dave, genuinely enjoyed being around Ken.

The last member of the gang was Todd Hamilton. Todd was the jock of the group. Short but powerfully built, he had been a multi-sport star in high school and a member of the football team at Lofdahl. Some people were unsure how to respond to Todd because he was intensely competitive and aggressive. But the gang knew how to handle Todd. Dave remembered the time when Landis called for Todd from a remote phone, pretending to be a national sports writer. Only when Ken and Dave could no longer contain their laughter was the ruse revealed.

Todd found his niche in sales. He recently received a big promotion and was now sales manager for a pharmaceutical company in Minneapolis. His wife, Penny, went back to school after they were unable to have children and she now served on the faculty of a local community college. Todd was a significant financial supporter of Dave and a zealous proponent of missions in general. He served as the missions committee chairman at his church and worked hard to keep abreast of significant issues in missions.

Dave could think of no better group of people with which to discuss new approaches to church planting. They were not only committed to the faith and enthusiastic about missions, but each of the men was also an innovative thinker. Dave knew innovation and "out of the box" thinking was an absolute necessity. He knew they would come—if they could. But *could* they come? Each had a demanding schedule.

His pulse accelerating, Dave composed an email briefly outlining the challenge. He entered their addresses and hit

THERE IS NO TIME

the Send button, offering a quick prayer that God would see fit to bring his dream to reality.

Within two hours, after a flurry of emails back and forth, the answer was clear. The gang would reunite for the first time since graduation. In a touching display of commitment to Dave, each man cleared his calendar. Todd even rescheduled a sales meeting on the east coast in order to attend. Wanting an offsite location where they would be undisturbed from normal, daily concerns, Landis offered his parents' cabin nestled in the mountains outside of Dillon, Colorado, as a place to meet. In just six weeks, the foursome would gather and together tackle Dave's dilemma.

6

REUNION

The intervening days could not fly by fast enough for Dave. While he relished the opportunity to hang out with his college buddies again, he was even more interested in gaining their input on a new model for church planting.

A careful coordination of flights into the Denver airport allowed them to all arrive within an hour of each other and share one rental car. When Dave arrived on his flight from Chicago, Landis and Todd were already there to greet him at his gate.

"Hey guys!" Dave shouted as soon as he cleared the crowd at the gate, waving with one hand and lugging his carry-on in the other.

"Look at the missionary!" Todd said, giving him a warm, hearty handshake. "You don't look too shabby for being a rebel hostage."

"You don't look too shabby yourself—except for that fuzz on your face." Dave shot back, noting Todd's newly grown goatee. It was a bit scraggly.

"I happen to like it. Penny does too. Makes me look more sophisticated."

"That's about like trying to dress a mule in a tuxedo." The harmless jabs that had marked their college days resumed as if the decade apart were nothing. Dave found himself amazed how quickly he felt comfortable with these guys. It felt good. Really good.

Landis piped in. "You really do look good, Dave. Either God has taken extraordinary care of you in Tognumou or your mother's cooking has agreed with you since you have come back."

"It's probably a little of both. God did graciously spare my life, but I would also have to say that the two months since my return has put a skip back in my step."

"And maybe a couple inches around your belt," joked Todd, pinching at Dave's midsection. Dave laughed. Todd always kept himself in peak physical condition, working out at the gym regularly. Dave felt no threat trying to keep up with him.

"When does Ken arrive?" Dave asked. Landis would know. He always knew those things.

"In about twenty minutes, but it is on a United flight at the other end of the terminal. We'd better start moving in that direction."

They took off down the terminal, dodging hurried passengers with rolling suitcases, staying three abreast, talking all the way. It didn't take long to get up to speed with each other.

When Ken got off the plane, the same ritual repeated itself. Greetings, handshakes, jokes, and even some hugs punctuated the first minutes together. Ken immediately added some spice to the group with his louder than normal laughter. Todd commented about Ken's receding hairline. Ken returned the favor by making an unflattering description of Todd's new facial hair. They joked and swapped stories all the way to the rental car counter and most of the way to the cabin. A few pictures of children circulated. Everything was kept light with sports, family news and church updates dominating the conversation. Dave knew there would be time to get into the main order of business later. At the moment, he simply reveled in the joy of being with his friends again.

The cabin was no shack, but then again, Dave didn't expect anything less than quality. Landis's family had been very successful in business and this was a treasured getaway location for them. It was perfect for the gang: a true log cabin with three spacious bedrooms and a hideaway sofa in the great room which boasted a vaulted ceiling opening up to a wall of windows and a deck with a spectacular view. The kitchen was already stocked with food, courtesy of the Martin family. Landis offered to use the sofa but Ken insisted he liked sleeping on such contraptions. Each of them stowed their gear quickly and Landis started firing up the grill on the deck. Tonight they would eat fine specimens from their favorite food group: steak!

7

THE DEFINING QUESTION

Dave was not sure what was better: eating a finely grilled New York strip or basking in the fellowship of loved friends. Since he enjoyed both at the moment, he knew he was experiencing rare air.

Todd gave a satisfied grunt, rubbed his full but well-defined belly and, rocking back in his deck chair, said to Dave, "So, it sounds like you want to explore ways to plant churches faster."

"Yes," replied Dave. "My time in Tognumou showed me that the increasing volatility of the world makes lengthy missionary tenures unlikely at best and impossible at worst. While there are some parts of the world that enjoy relative stability, the most unreached areas are the most unstable. I know personally the frustration of being forced out of a field before a church is even close to maturity. While missionary work may be possible in that land sometime in the future, it caused me to ask myself what I could have done differently to move the church along faster."

"But isn't cross-cultural church planting a slow business?" asked Ken. "You were working in a hardcore Muslim country."

"Right. I understand there may be different levels of receptivity with various groups. But that does not give us an excuse to think it has to take an entire lifetime to plant a church. Frankly, in today's world you probably don't have that much time," said Dave.

Todd jumped in. "How do you know it can be done any faster?"

"I don't. But I did a study of Paul's missionary journeys in the book of Acts. He planted churches very quickly. Sometimes he was naming elders after just a few months."

"But you are not the Apostle Paul," Ken interjected.

"No, I am not. Far from it." Dave smiled and leaned forward toward his friends. "But what I *did* see is that God is able to establish mature churches at a rapid pace. I know it can be done because it has been done in the past and God has not lost one ounce of His power. Furthermore, I am left without an adequate answer to a compelling question."

"What question is that?" asked Todd.

"Why wouldn't God want to plant churches quickly today?"

The rapid-fire conversation stopped suddenly with those words as each of them pondered a response. *Why wouldn't God desire that churches be rapidly planted in the twenty-first century?*

"You've got a good point, Dave," Landis finally spoke. Dave appreciated those words because he knew Landis had a razor-sharp mind.

Landis continued. "Logically, if God did not want to

plant churches quickly, then that would necessarily mean He had less concern or love for the lost people of the world today. Certainly there is no question the need for the church to flourish is greater than ever because there are more unsaved people alive today than at any other time in history. Furthermore, trends show population growth continues to outstrip the growth of the church. Each year we are falling further behind. Therefore, if God did not want to plant churches more quickly, then it would mean God cared more for the people of the first century than He does for the people of the twenty-first century."

"But theologically, we know that is not true," Ken added.

"Right. God's love for man is unchanging just as His entire character is unchanging," Landis said.

"So…what now?" Todd looked around the circle.

"We are left with no reason to believe God would not want to establish mature churches as rapidly as He did in the first century," Landis spoke slowly but with assurance.

"That is precisely the conclusion I came to," Dave exclaimed. "We have to believe God wants to do this. We already believe God *can* do this. And, in light of the turmoil of the world today, we also believe it is *necessary* to do this."

"Whoa, Dave. You know what you are saying?" Todd mused. "You are talking about creating a new way of doing church planting!"

"Yep! But that is why I wanted you here. This is bigger than me and it will require more brainpower than I can muster up."

"But we're not missionaries! I love missions, but my training is in other areas," countered Todd.

"That is another reason I wanted you here. I suspect that

to really do this, it will take significant input from many different disciplines. Your training is a plus, not a negative."

Everyone stared at their dinner plates for a few moments, deep in thought.

Finally Landis broke the silence. "All right guys, we know what we have to do. And I somehow think God will give us the wisdom to do this if we ask Him." The others slowly nodded their heads.

"Yeah, but I don't do any heavy mental lifting without first having a big bowl of ice cream," joked Todd as he jumped from the table and headed for the kitchen.

"Sounds good to me," said Ken. "Ice cream, a good night's rest and we will get after it in the morning."

A cheer went up from the group and they left the deck as the first beams of moonlight cascaded across the star-filled sky.

8

THE FAITH CONTEXT

Dave's night was restless as his mind kept racing. What new insights would the day bring? Would there even be new insights? Anticipation coupled with anxiety allowed him little sleep.

After a breakfast of pancakes and scrambled eggs prepared by Ken, the four men gathered on the deck to start brainstorming. It was a crystal clear morning and the view resembled a postcard. Armed with notepads, pens, full stomachs, plenty of coffee and fresh air, the group was ready for action.

Ken launched out first. "Guys, it seems to me the place to start is by identifying the things we know are true about God and His Word which serve as a theological foundation for the church-planting process. We touched on some of these last night, but I think it would be good to formally affirm them. In a sense, you could call these the 'faith context' in which missions operates."

"Such as...?" asked Todd.

"Such as the power of the Gospel," said Dave. "Missionaries all believe in a powerful Gospel that is able to transform lives."

"Like the Apostle Paul talked about in Romans 1:16," added Todd. "I am not ashamed of the Gospel, because it is the power of God for the salvation of everyone who believes."

"That's not the only place Paul talks about the power of the Gospel message," said Ken. "He uses the same word in I Corinthians 2:4 and I Thessalonians 1:5. It's a consistent theme in his writings."

"So, what does all this mean for the church-planting missionary?" asked Todd.

Dave answered, "It means that we go out with confidence. For we know that the Gospel is inherently powerful and God has promised to use it to bring to faith those He is drawing to salvation. So, success is not dependent upon our skill or lack of it. Success is resident in a powerful Gospel message."

"I like that," said Todd. He drew a big circle and labeled it 'Faith Context'. Then, at the top of the circle, he wrote in the words: **Power of the Gospel**.

"That's a good start. What else is in this faith context?"

Landis entered the discussion for the first time. He leaned forward and said, "Something I have been thinking about is the amazing way God is able to facilitate His work. It's His ability to transcend logistical barriers and cause things to happen which naturally would not happen. Or his ability to connect people that otherwise would never get connected."

"What do you mean?" asked Todd.

"I mean what you see happen in Acts 8. You know the story. An Ethiopian eunuch is riding in his chariot, reading about the suffering servant from the prophet Isaiah, but not understanding what it says. Suddenly God propels Philip, who had been ministering in Samaria, to run up and join this chariot. The eunuch invites Philip to join him and Philip explains to him how the text refers to Jesus. The eunuch believes and is immediately baptized."

"I see what you are saying," said Ken. "But that's not the only example. The Bible is loaded with stories of God going before His servants and causing them to connect with the right people at the right time. "

"Agreed," interjected Todd. "But how does that relate to church planting?"

Dave piped up, "It has everything to do with church planting! For as we seek to establish new churches in unreached areas, we have to believe God is going to go before us and put us in contact with those who will not only come to faith in Christ but also be influential in reaching others for Christ. In other words, from our side, it may look like a chance encounter, but from God's side we know it is a display of His divine sovereignty."

"So, what do we call this?" asked Todd. "What do I write in my circle?"

"How about 'divine serendipity'?" offered Ken.

"Divine serendipity? Do those words even go together? What kind of heretic are you, preacher man?" exclaimed Todd.

"Hear me out. I know this sounds odd coming from someone with my training, but I think it accurately captures the truth we have described. 'Serendipity' communicates the fact of having fortuitous things happen on a regular basis. But by calling it 'divine' serendipity, we are acknowledging God is the one causing these fortuitous events to take place. It's a clever way of describing the tension between human responsibility and divine sovereignty. It's divine … serendipity."

The whole group mentally chewed on those words for a few seconds, filtering the terms through their theological systems. Then Landis said, "I like it. It's catchy. It's memorable. And it *is* the truth."

"Fine with me," Todd said. And he added **Divine Serendipity** to his faith context circle.

"Well, what else? Are there other entries that need to

appear in our faith context?" Todd inquired.

"I think so," said Ken. "We talk about the power of the Gospel, which is vital. And we acknowledge His sovereignty in causing things to happen in a fortuitous way. But, it is still more than that. For believing God can plant churches faster also requires we trust His ability to accomplish remarkable things. You see, it is one thing to believe in a powerful Gospel, but it is quite another to believe God can perform everything that is necessary to establish a mature church in a relatively short period of time."

"I know I am still struggling to fully embrace that," said Dave. "I see it happening in the Word, but part of me still pushes to confine those awesome works of God to a different age. Therefore, I don't expect God to do amazing things."

"I can identify with you, Dave," replied Ken. "Yet, at the same time, Paul was clear to us in Ephesians 3:20 that God is able to do immeasurably more than all we ask or imagine, according to his power that is at work within us. So, while God may not choose to work in amazing ways in every circumstance, we must have a firm belief God can do this."

"So, God is able to plant churches quickly," said Todd.

"And God is able to raise up capable leaders in a short period of time," added Dave.

"And God is able to guide the church even when the missionaries are gone," said Ken, "Even supplying all that it needs in terms of resources from within the new church."

"So, let's add it to our chart."

Todd added **God's Ability** to the circle.

"So, our faith context consists of three elements so far: the Power of the Gospel, Divine Serendipity and God's Ability. Is that sufficient? Or, is there anything else that still needs to be added?"

After a brief pause, Dave spoke up. "There is one more. Again, I have been giving this a lot of thought, and something else that must appear here is the primacy of prayer. As you know, the Apostle Paul was the consummate missionary. He had gifts that far outstrip mine. And yet, when you read through his letters, he is constantly asking people to pray for him. Sometimes he asked his readers to pray that he would have boldness, which is sobering to me because I always considered him to be fearless. But other times, such as in Colossians 4, he asked them to pray God would give him open doors." Turning quickly in his Bible, Dave read the words of Colossians 4:2-4, "Devote yourselves to prayer, being watchful and thankful. And pray for us, too, that God may open a door for our message, so that we may proclaim the mystery of Christ, for which I am in chains. Pray that I may proclaim it clearly, as I should."

Dave continued. "That tells me if we want to see churches planted faster, then it is absolutely essential we have a whole army of prayer warriors who are committed to daily intercession, pleading with God to open doors for the Gospel."

"While that's obvious, it is so neglected today," said Ken. "We give lip service to prayer, but we spend precious little time in fervent prayer mostly because we fail to recognize the strategic role it has in opening new doors for God's Word. We somehow think we can, through our brilliant schemes and plans, pry open these doors that have been closed. The fact is, we can't. We can only pray them open."

"And then we wonder why it takes so long to plant a church," said Todd. "It may be rooted in an abysmal prayer effort."

"There is another verse that I cannot get out of my mind on this subject, and that is 2 Thessalonians 3:1," Dave noted. "Paul writes to this blue-ribbon church that was making exceptional progress in the faith and says, 'pray for us that the message of the Lord may spread rapidly and be honored, just as it was with you.' I did a word study on the verb *spread rapidly* and found out that the root means literally 'to run'. It seems to indicate that if we want the Gospel to run freely and spread quickly through a region, then we have to bathe such efforts in prayer."

"And that is what we want to see happen in church planting," said Todd again. "We want to see the Gospel spread like wildfire. So, let me add **Primacy of Prayer** to my chart."

Dave took a look at the sheet and then nodded his head in tacit approval. "None of this would qualify us as raging revolutionaries. It's all basic stuff. But putting it down on paper like this serves to reinforce it in my mind. I do believe in the power of the Gospel. I do believe in divine serendipity. I do believe in God's ability to produce God-sized results and in the primacy of prayer. But while I believe those things, I often act like I have never heard of those truths before."

"You mean, like forgetting how powerful the Gospel message is?" asked Ken.

"Yes, but not only that. During my time in Tognumou, I would also question whether it was even possible that the Fonu could ever financially sustain a church. I found myself thinking that they would always have to be dependent upon funds from the West."

"That's understandable," offered Landis. "It is a subsistence culture."

"But that is no excuse to doubt God's ability to provide all the church needs from within the church itself. This chart reminds me I cannot do that. If I am going to plant churches faster, I have to keep all of these truths from the faith context in my mind."

Dave's frank admission caused a brief lull in the conversation. While he had confessed his shortcomings in this area, everyone else knew they had experienced the same doubts.

Finally Todd, with a mischievous grin on his face, broke the silence. "Okay—break time! I will give my helping of dessert tonight to anyone who thinks they can whip me in ping pong!"

"Consider yourself to be fasting, my friend," boasted Ken. "I can taste your dessert right now." With that challenge, the foursome quickly broke from their deck chairs and hurriedly made their way to the lower level of the cabin for some recreation.

9

THE 'WHY' QUESTION

After a raucous hour playing ping pong, the foursome returned to the task at hand. Landis startled the others by saying, "Guys—I fear we are missing something here. Something very important. We have not answered the 'why' question. At least, not sufficiently. I know why Dave wants to do this. He was frustrated in leaving a work that was unfinished in Tognumou. But the reason for rolling out a new approach to cross-cultural church planting has to transcend one man's disappointing experience. That would never fly in the corporate world. It has to be more compelling with much more rationale."

"The same thing crossed my mind," chimed in Todd. "I like the progress we have made, but if I were trying to sell this to a skeptical client, I would need some convincing reasons why he should try my new product."

"Exactly! Just because we are dealing with a sanctified audience does not mean that we can be sloppy in our thinking."

"So, let's back the truck up and answer the 'why' question. And here is the way I would word it: Why do we need to find a way to establish churches faster?"

The question sent brain cells spinning.

After a few moments, Dave plopped his legal pad on the table. "Well, it seems obvious one of the reasons we need to try new approaches is because of the increasing volatility of the world. I did some research in this area when I was forced out prematurely from Tognumou. In 1960, there were about ten major armed conflicts present in the world. That may seem like a lot, but by 2000, that number had almost increased four-fold. So, it not only seems to us that countries are more unstable today, it can be easily documented. And the most alarming fact I uncovered was that the vast majority of these armed conflicts are in the most unreached parts of the world. Therefore, if we want to plant churches where the need is the greatest, we will have to set up shop in these precarious cultures."

The furrows on Ken's brow showed he was pondering what had been said. "You know, this is not contrary to how Jesus said it would be. Wars and rumors of wars. Hostility. Instability. Honestly, we should not be surprised."

"I don't know if surprise is accurate. We may not be totally surprised but that doesn't mean that we have adjusted our plans to fit the reality of the world scene."

"Right!" said Todd. "And consequently, we continue with methods and assumptions that don't reflect the fact the world has changed."

"And is continuing to change—faster and faster. Like a top spinning out of control," added Landis.

"So what we are saying is that sociopolitical realities

no longer afford us the luxury of assuming we can stay as missionaries in a country for thirty or forty uninterrupted years. In rare instances that may be true, but as a general rule the doors to these unreached countries open and close very quickly," said Dave. "Therefore, when the opportunity presents itself, we have to be agile enough to seize it immediately and effective enough to establish a church quickly, knowing we probably have only a limited amount of time to get the job done. My experience in Tognumou is the perfect example. For decades there had been peace and stability in the country. Then, suddenly, the whole nation erupts in civil war forcing all the foreigners from the land. Unfortunately, that same scenario is being repeated over and over again all around the world."

Todd nodded, picked up his pen and wrote the words **Sociopolitical Realities** on his paper.

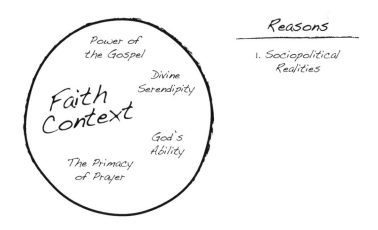

"Okay, I've got it down. The first compelling reason for finding a way to plant churches faster is because this world is in turmoil and rapidly changing political scenes require us to find new models. Makes sense to me. Why else is this necessary?"

There was a momentary pause in the conversation. Ken uncoiled from his chair, taking a stand with his back to the group. Then, he turned to face them. "I know of another reason. It's a reason that, in a sense has been true since the early church, but is even more true today."

"What is it?" asked Todd.

"The imminent return of Christ.

"Now, hear me out. We all believe in the imminent return of Jesus Christ. It is something we have been taught from our childhood. It is a truth deeply embedded in the New Testament. As a pastor and theologian, I have often taught it to others. However, the urgency inherent in that truth often fails to be reflected in our daily lives. Or, in this case, in our church-planting strategy. In other words, I am saying if we truly believe Christ's return is imminent—that it could come any day—and if we also believe every passing day brings us one day closer to that climactic event, then that should necessarily cause us to shed complacency and move with haste. For we do not have forever to get the job done!"

"You're preachin' now," chuckled Todd. "Bring it, preacher! Bring it!"

"I know what you are saying," added Landis. "There is often an unfortunate disconnect between our theology and our practice. We believe in imminency and yet we live like we don't think Jesus is coming back for another hundred years—or more."

"Which may be true," said Dave.

"But it may not be true," responded Landis. "James says 'the Judge is right at the door.' The imagery of that verse tells us our Lord may break through into time and space at any moment."

"I guess the question we need to honestly ask ourselves is, if we knew for sure Jesus was returning in just six months, would that change our strategy?" As Ken asked this question it was obvious he was chewing on the answer. "And if it *would* change our strategy, then the painful follow-up question is, Why aren't we doing that now?"

"I get your point." Dave was also standing now. "But isn't that somewhat artificial? The fact is Christ has delayed His return already almost two thousand years. During that whole time believers have been expecting His return but it hasn't happened. What makes us think there is reason for more urgency now?"

"I admit it's dangerous to jump to conclusions based on world events," Ken responded. "We all know plenty of apocalyptic-like things have happened in recent years. Terrorist attacks. Earthquakes. Hurricanes. But this earth has always witnessed a steady stream of cataclysmic events. It's part of the curse."

"So why more urgency now?"

"Two reasons. First, because it represents a biblical perspective that we, as believers, are to hold. We cannot expect the rest of the world to be thinking we are approaching the climactic moment in human history. But we have received God's revelation in this area. We know it is coming. So, our actions and attitudes should reflect that knowledge."

"Secondly, each passing day brings us one day closer to that reality. So, today we are nearer to His return than we have ever been. Tomorrow we will be even nearer. Therefore, the urgency is not artificial. It is real."

"You're right, Ken," Dave conceded after more thought.

"The Imminent Return of Christ must be one of the reasons that pushes us to plant churches faster."

"Okay. I have it down," said Todd, as he jotted it on the paper. "Are there any other reasons we should find a new approach to church planting?"

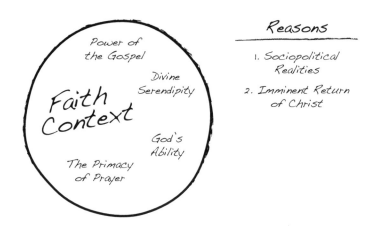

"I have another one." Ken was still standing like a teacher in a classroom. "I guess you could call it a numerical reason. But I have been doing some research on the web about population growth. And I have been comparing it to the growth of the evangelical church worldwide. And it is plain to see we are not keeping up."

"Let me show you what I found. According to the people who keep track of these things, around 137 million people are born into this world every year. That is over four persons every second. Around 56 million people die every year. That means that the net gain in the world population is presently about 80 or 81 million people annually.

"The evangelical church is growing in the world,

46

somewhere between 4.5 and 4.7 percent a year. While that is encouraging, it is not keeping up with the population growth of the world. So that means every day we are falling further behind. It means each new day there are more unbelievers alive than at any other time in history. It means that, while our current methods have produced a global church for the first time since the church was born, we are not keeping up. So, we need to explore ways to spawn faster spiritual reproduction."

Todd jumped in, "I read somewhere a quote by Oswald Sanders: 'Men are born and die whether or not Christians are ready to give them the Gospel. And hence, if the church of any generation does not evangelize the heathen of that generation, those heathen will never be evangelized at all.' If so, then we have the responsibility for evangelizing this generation."

"And we are not keeping up. That does not mean our methods were wrong in the past. But it does mean we need to try and find new ways to reach a generation that is seemingly expanding at an exponential rate," replied Ken.

Landis gave an analogy. "In the manufacturing world, we would almost call this a crisis. Let's say you had an assembly line that was making 100,000 widgets a day. However, let's say that you had an inadequate distribution system and could only ship 75,000 widgets a day. That means each day you are adding another 25,000 widgets to the pile. But the big difference is, in a business you can regulate the flow of the widgets on the assembly line to match distribution capability. However, that is not possible here. So, the number of unsaved people that need to be reached for Christ continues to grow and grow every single day."

That sobering thought brought silence among the four

friends. Todd added the words **Numerical Growth—Not Keeping Up** to his list.

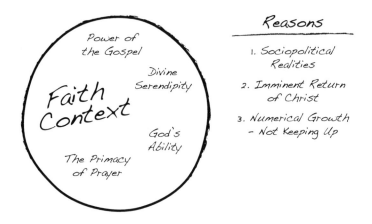

Landis was not done. "There is one more reason I want to add to our list. It is one I have pondered often."

"What is it?" Dave was curious.

"Let's call it 'stewardship'. And I want to be kind here, but I also need to be honest." Because Landis was always measured with his words, the other three paid him close attention.

Landis continued, "As you well know, God has blessed my extended family with significant material resources. As a result, my parents have always had the joy and ability to make sizeable contributions from their family foundation to the Lord's work, including the support of missionaries."

His face stiffened as he carefully chose his words. "When they gave, they gave as an investment. Only, instead of realizing gains in this present world, they knew they were realizing rewards in eternity. However, any investment requires a return. It looks for results. In other words, it requires that you ask, Am I gaining the return on my investment that I desire here? In the financial world, that is easy to measure. In the spiritual world, however, that can be more difficult to assess. And I guess what I am saying is, missions and missionaries need to be more mindful of the concept of return on investment."

Dave became defensive. He blurted out, "Landis, are you saying missionaries need to produce a certain number of converts in order to justify their existence? Because if you are, you are ignoring the difficulty of the work in many parts of the world!"

"No, I am not saying that. But I am saying missions has a reputation of placing a higher value on faithfulness and activity than on actual results. I am a fan of faithfulness. I do not want to support unfaithful missionaries. However, the Great Commission is ultimately about results. Jesus said, 'Go therefore and make disciples of all the nations.' And it sometimes appears missionaries, in all their labors, can lose sight of the goal and not give sufficient attention to results."

Todd was now fully engaged in the discussion. His work in sales caused him to see some parallels. "I know exactly what you are saying. As a sales manager, I often will be working with a new salesperson that can provide me with an impressive call list and prospecting activity. But the bottom line would be very unimpressive. A lot of activity but very few sales."

"So, do you fire the salesperson? Do you axe him even though he has been obviously working hard?" asked Dave, still a little agitated.

"No. You don't question people's heart or work ethic. They

obviously work hard. But you do question their strategy and methods. You see, if something isn't working, it is foolish to think it will suddenly start working if you just keep doing it. So, if you are not having success with your current approach, the solution is obvious: change your approach."

Landis jumped back in, seeking to further reassure Dave. "You see, if you have a focus on results, which is demanded by stewardship, you also have to be constantly evaluating your methods to see if they are bringing the results you want."

"And evaluating your methods means establishing ways to measure progress," added Todd. "In other words, it is like a scoreboard at a basketball game. At a game, I can look at the scoreboard at anytime during the game and see if my team is on track to accomplish their goal, which is to win the game. The scoreboard will tell me if they are ahead or behind. And if they are behind, I would expect the coach to be making changes in his team strategy to hopefully alter the outcome."

"And that is my main point," said Landis. "Along with my family, I invest in missions and missionaries because I am interested in achieving the final goal, which is to see people from every tribe and tongue worshiping the Lamb in eternity. Since I am giving of my resources to that end, I know this is my opportunity to gain eternal reward—which is much more attractive to me than temporary material gain. However, it seems the mission community does not always understand this results focus. For a giver, this is all I have. I am giving part of my life, what I have earned, to invest in Kingdom work and lay hold of rewards in the future. But if the results never materialize due to sloppy strategy or a failure to evaluate the effectiveness of methods, then my reward also does not materialize. So, often times, I will continue to financially support a missionary because of my relationship with him or her, while lamenting the lack of careful evaluation and an inattention to results."

Dave felt attacked now. "Was that true of me, Landis? Did you feel I was not a good investment? Because I probably did not produce your 'bottom line'!"

"Dave, this is not personal. I am talking now in general terms, across the entire industry. Generally speaking, the North American church is not impressed with the results gained by missionaries today. But they don't question their faithfulness or commitment. They only question whether strategy and methods are evaluated often enough in order to gain the best results in the desired time frame."

"How come no one has ever told me this before?" Dave was obviously wounded.

"I guess you could call it one of those 'sacred cows' that exist in the church today." Ken had now entered the debate. "There are many times I have thought these very thoughts. I read the prayer letters of our missionaries. I get the email updates. Some speak specifically of the results they are seeing, but more often they are filled with reports of busyness and activity, even to the point of fatigue. I knew I would be branded unspiritual or anti-missions if I voiced my concerns. So, I choked them back and stayed silent. But the whispers remain."

"This is why this discussion is so needed," added Todd quietly. "We need to find a way for missionaries to provide a better return on investment and start churches faster. Not in twenty years or forty years. But in ten or eight or five."

Dave stayed silent. In his heart, he knew they were right. But how? How could he establish a mature church faster?

Tomorrow he would find out.

THE CORE

Early the next morning, Ken noticed Dave hugging a steaming coffee cup in a quiet corner of the deck. The red rays of the sun were just beginning to rip through the crisp mountain air.

"How'ya doing?" asked Ken, putting a warm hand on his shoulder.

Dave smiled and took another sip from his brew. "I'm fine—I guess. I cannot deny the talk last night stung a little. But that is why I wanted you guys here—to be honest with me. I worked through it all during the night and I know you are right. So, I am ready to get after it today!"

Ken replied, "Great! I think we are going to have a good day."

Dave could tell his concern was genuine.

Ken started to turn away but Dave stopped him. "But Ken, make me a promise—no more sacred cows! Okay?"

"Okay. But you make me a promise—no more loud

snoring like a freight train! Good grief. I thought you were going to shatter the window panes last night!"

Dave yelped in protest but before he could defend himself any more, Ken slipped out of his grasp and with a mischievous laugh joined the other two around a table heaped with biscuits and gravy.

"Todd, let's review what we have so far." Landis had put on his executive hat and was commandeering the process.

Todd rustled through his papers and then, in a voice sounding strangely similar to a news anchor, read to the group. "All right, we first established the faith context in which missions operates. Putting them on a chart, we listed four elements: first, the power of the Gospel; second, divine serendipity; third, God's ability; and lastly, the primacy of prayer. Then, last night, we answered the 'why' question and listed four reasons why we needed to find a way to plant churches faster. The first reason was sociopolitical. That is, the increasing political turmoil in the world requires that we move with speed and efficiency. The second reason was theological. We said the imminent return of Christ shows we don't have forever to get this job done. The third reason was numerical. Despite the growth of the church, we are not keeping up with population growth so we falling further behind. And the last reason was stewardship. Pursuing efficiency and results shows we want to be good stewards of the resources entrusted to us.

The whole group listened intently to the summary, nodding in agreement with the words.

"That's a good beginning," lamented Ken. "But now we have the hard work. Now we have to discover and define this new church-planting model. The question I have been pondering is, What would accelerate the work? Is it different training? Is it different people? Is it different strategy?"

"It obviously means we make a radical departure from more traditional methods because they are rooted in longevity and deep acculturation," added Dave. "Those methods produce results, as we know, but they also take time."

"But not all that time is productive time." Ken was speaking again, reflecting on his experience as a pastor. "From talking to the missionaries supported by my church, and from my own visits to the field, it is apparent a certain percentage of each day is devoted to activity that does not move the church-planting process forward. Not wrong things—just things unrelated to the task at hand. And sometimes, it can appear the whole process can get stalled out for long periods of time. If we are going to build a new method, we somehow have to address that issue."

Landis jumped in. "Guys, I have three ideas to put on the table. First, have any of you heard of 'lean thinking'?" Three shaking heads indicated that they had not.

"It's a process used in the manufacturing world which maps the value stream and identifies when value is added to the product. It also then identifies when time or material is wasted. This is called 'muda'."

"Muda?" Todd laughed. "Why is it called muda?"

"That's a Japanese word for *waste*," replied Landis. "The Japanese are the ones who invented lean thinking. It was started by Toyota in the car manufacturing world. They ended up revolutionizing the whole industry by making the assembly line more efficient. As a result, they not only cut costs but they also dramatically increased production. Since then everyone else has followed their lead."

"But that is a manufacturing process," said Dave. "We are talking about planting churches, not making cars. Why do you think this lean thinking can be applied to church planting?"

"Because this can apply to any process, even if your product is a mature church and not a Mercedes. Every process, whether aimed at a tangible product or an intangible one, can be mapped for a value stream and every process has waste in it. Therefore, in the church-planting process, we identify at what points value is added, and also identify when waste occurs. The goal then would be to eliminate the waste and move as swiftly as possible from point to point where value is added. Ken, you admitted that there are times when the church-planting process doesn't seem to move forward much with your missionaries, right? Lean thinking allows you to study the process, see why the waste occurs and then change the process so it doesn't happen again."

Ken interrupted, "But do you have to hold an MBA to understand how to implement lean thinking?"

"Not at all. In fact, in many companies, the ones who see waste the clearest and make the best suggestions are the front-line workers in a factory. If they can do this, then so can your typical missionary."

"Makes sense to me," Todd interjected. "I think I would love to see how lean thinking could help make my work more efficient."

"It also represents the kind of perspective that we need to consider if we are truly going to put together a new church-planting model," added Dave.

Landis continued. "Second, in addition to lean thinking, I think church planting needs to incorporate principles from Continuous Quality Improvement."

"What does that mean?" asked Todd.

"Well, it is another science that was mastered by Toyota. It means you are always looking at ways to improve yourself and your processes. It means you are never satisfied with your progress. It means you are you constantly reading, learning and growing so that you might find fresh ideas that can help you get better at what you do."

Ken jumped in. "In the case of church planting, we don't become complacent while we are discovering ways to shorten the process. We must continue to drive ahead in the quality improvement cycle and still search for new breakthroughs. It means the entire organization becomes a learning organization."

"Exactly," said Landis. "Because Toyota took this approach, not only did they discover more efficient ways to produce cars, but they also found ways to make cars that are consistently considered tops in quality for the industry. So, efficiency does not mean you sacrifice quality. You can become better at how you do something—your processes—AND better at what you produce."

Todd laughed. "I knew there was a reason I liked to drive Toyotas!"

"But there is more." Landis was not finished. "If we want to plant churches faster, then thirdly, we must think teams, not just individuals."

Dave felt another sacred cow entering the room. "What do you mean?"

"I mean missions has historically valued the rugged missionary pioneer who would trek deep into the bush to start a church. Because they were all by themselves, they had to be omni-gifted. They had to be evangelist, preacher, contractor, school teacher and medical doctor all rolled into one."

Dave knew exactly what he meant. As a solo missionary laboring among the Fonu people, he had to wear all the hats. He was skilled at some tasks—unskilled at others.

Landis continued, "As much as a gifted individual can accomplish, a team can always accomplish more—because synergy develops on a team. It is this synergy that causes a team to be more than the sum of its parts. To put it in another way, a team will always accomplish more than any group of individuals."

Dave began shaking his head, "I don't know, Landis. I have heard some real horror stories about teams. It seems like teams spend more energy fighting than they do addressing the task at hand. Especially on the mission field when culture shock hits."

"There is no question conflict can happen on a team.

But I suspect none of your examples were real teams. They were probably just work groups."

"But we always called them a team. What's the difference?"

"There is a huge difference, Dave! Most work that is accomplished in the world is done by work groups. A work group is just a collection of people, usually led by a supervisor, who may be working toward a common goal but who do completely individualistic work. So, they don't have to cooperate or collaborate but can just do their jobs. An example of this would be any kind of factory assembly line. Each person on the line does his job, but the individuals on the line don't have to work together."

Ken jumped in. "I know what that looks like. My father worked at a job just like that in a steel mill for nearly forty years."

"And most mission agencies may refer to their missionaries on a particular field as a team, but they are not. They are just a work group." Landis was pressing his point.

"I suppose you are right," Dave replied. "Most of the missionaries with our agency in my part of the world had individual ministries. We came together occasionally for prayer and fellowship, but our daily lives and work did not require us to intersect. But we got things done!"

"No doubt good work was accomplished! Like I said, most work that is accomplished in the world is done by work groups. However, I will go back to what I said a few minutes ago—a real team will always accomplish more than any collection of individuals. Therefore, if we want to establish churches faster, it seems to me we have to start with a team—not a work group."

"So...what does a real team look like?" Todd's question

revealed his increasing interest.

"Well, let me share what we have found out in our training of teams in my company. First, teams have to be carefully selected. In other words, for teams to function properly, you must have the right skill sets present. In the case of a church-planting team, you would probably want someone gifted in administration, another who was an evangelist, another who was skilled in teaching and discipleship, and so on. You see, the beauty of a team is that you can operate in the area of your strengths and not your weaknesses."

"I see it as a microcosm of how God puts together the Body of Christ," said Ken. "We are all parts of the Body and we are all needed in the Body but we are to function in the area of our giftedness to the edification of the Body."

"Exactly! A team is a miniature representation of that. Team members are placed on a particular team based upon their skill sets and giftedness," added Landis.

"So, how big should a team be?" Dave asked.

"Well, there are a number of determining factors. However, most experts say the ideal range is seven to twelve members. If you get smaller than that, you can have gaps in your team giftedness, and if you get larger than that, team dynamics can become overly cumbersome."

Landis continued, "Secondly, teams share a common purpose or goal. That is, they have identified and have committed themselves to reaching a certain objective. And they have agreed upon how they are going to go about reaching that objective."

Now Todd spoke up. "That was true of my football team at Lofdahl. Our objective was to move the football down the field and hopefully score a touchdown. But to do that, on every play, everyone had a job to do. The center had to hike the ball on the right count and block the nose tackle. The quarterback had to cleanly receive the snap and make an accurate pitch to me as the running back. Each lineman had an assignment, which was designed to open a hole in the defense. And then I had to field the pitch, find the hole and get as much yardage as possible without coughing up the pigskin."

"And what if someone didn't do his job?" asked Landis.

"It wasn't good! In most cases, a busted play would result in lost yardage or even a turnover."

"If I remember right, didn't you lead the league in fumbles?" roared Ken, causing the whole group, except Todd, to erupt in laughter.

"Not exactly! But there were far too many times when there was an ugly defensive tackle staring at me just after I received the ball." Wanting to quickly change the subject, Todd asked, "Is there more to being a real team? More than just selection and a common purpose?"

"Well, thirdly, there is the practice of the disciplines that must characterize a team. Such as trust and mutual accountability. Most teams, if they fail, do so because of a lack of trust. They don't trust each other and consequently, fail to be real with each other or buy into the goals of the team."

Dave wanted clarification. "This sounds like you cannot form a real team on the field. This sounds like you have to select and train a team before they go to the field."

Landis answered, "While it would not be impossible to do team training on the field, factors there would complicate it. However, the key is not the location of the training but the fact that the entire team is trained as a team. Therefore, you cannot add someone to the team unless the team is retrained to understand, incorporate and trust the new member."

"That is radically different from how we operate today," said Dave. "People are normally committed to a field, not a team. The personnel on the field can change dramatically over the course of just a few years. It would necessarily mean we stop sending people to a field and start sending teams to a field."

"I understand this would completely change the organizational paradigm of a mission agency. But I return to our task at hand—and that is to find a way to plant churches faster. In my eyes, it has to start with a carefully selected, well-trained team of missionaries."

"A team of missionaries who understands lean thinking!" added Todd. "Because **Team** is at the core, I am going to put it in the middle of our diagram." He added it to the drawing.

Dave looked at the diagram and reflected on his own experience. A team. A *real* team. Things were suddenly getting interesting.

11

SHORTENING THE CYCLE

Todd wrapped his hands around a dirt-brown mug filled with a piping hot cappuccino. He had a quizzical look on his face. "What are we going to call this?" he asked, looking at the team diagram on the paper. He slurped another mouthful of the delicious concoction. "I am a salesman. And therefore, I know if you are going to sell this to someone else, you have to put a label on it. You know, some kind of a title that describes the process we are talking about."

"You know, Todd's right," added Ken. "If we expect churches and missions committees to buy in to this, we have to fly a flag over it."

"So, what is it? Is this a church-planting version of Jiffy-Lube?" Todd deadpanned. "Or, is this a McDonaldization of missions? You know, McMissions?"

"Be careful here," remarked Landis. "You can cheapen the product if you slap the wrong moniker on it. And you can also communicate the wrong image to people. This is not like fast food, because no one would argue that a burger joint and a fine steak house produce the same quality of fare. But our goal is to produce the same product—a mature, reproducing church. We just want to do it faster."

The foursome all sat quietly for a moment, pondering a solution. Finally Ken spoke up. "How about something that describes the process? We are talking about church planting that has a shorter overall cycle to it from beginning to end. So what about 'Shorter Cycle Church Planting'?" Ken was spelling it out like he was casting a vision before an executive team.

Todd jumped in, "I think you are on to something. But I would change the word *shorter* because that is a comparative and it always begs the question, Shorter than what? How about just 'Short-Cycle Church Planting'? It is a cycle, just like in traditional missions. But it is a short cycle."

"Would that get confused with short-term missions?" asked Ken.

"Maybe. But if you get a chance to explain it, complete with the team concept and lean thinking, people will quickly see you are talking about a different animal."

"Okay. I can live with it," added Dave. "Let's call it Short-Cycle Church Planting—at least for right now."

"It starts with a team," Todd rehearsed. "But then what? While training a real team to do church planting represents a genuine departure from the past, we have to go farther than that. What principles will this team use to establish a mature church faster?"

Dave was already primed for this question. "Well, I know one principle that needs to be part of the equation. I would call it simultaneous activity."

"What do you mean by that, Dave?" asked Landis. "Is

that like multitasking?"

"No, not at all. Simultaneous activity is to be contrasted to sequential activity. Missionaries are conditioned to thinking in a sequence when it comes to church planting. We first learn the language. Then we spend time utilizing those language skills to develop relationships with people. Then we capitalize on those relationships and seek to share the Gospel. Then we build into the converts and disciple them. Then we start to gather the disciples into a group and start a church. Then we develop leaders to lead the church. Then, we take a group and seek to start the whole process over again. It all makes logical sense, but it is deadly to what we are calling 'Short-Cycle Church Planting'."

"Why?" asked Todd.

"Because the assumption is that you cannot progress to the next phase until you have satisfactorily completed the previous phase. It's like watching a long freight train pass by. You can't get to the end of the train unless you watch each car go by. Likewise, in a sequential, linear mindset, you can't get to the end of the church-planting process unless you have properly passed through each of the prescribed phases of a church plant."

"And that takes time," observed Ken.

"And it is time that is loaded with 'muda'," added Todd.

"So, as I have given this some thought, I have decided that simultaneous activity is better than sequential activity. For in simultaneous activity you are combining steps in the process. It means you don't wait to learn the language before you start to share the Gospel. Even though you may have limited language skills, you start sowing the seed from day one. And it means you don't wait until you have a group of converts before you begin developing leaders. Instead, you start looking for key leaders and influencers from the very beginning. It may seem like a subtle distinction to you, but it is a huge difference in mindset. It means that at any time in the church-planting process, you could be involved in any phase of the church-planting process without necessarily having passed through all the other phases."

Todd chimed in. "This may seem like a silly example, but I see the difference you are describing like the difference between a VHS tape and a DVD."

Ken roared. "You *still* have a VCR, Todd?" The group laughed loudly.

"Yes I do! I keep it in the basement to watch old homemade movies. But hear me out! Sequential activity is like watching a VHS tape. The only way you can get to the end of the tape is to play the tape all the way through. Simultaneous activity is like watching a DVD. You can pull up the menu and skip to any part of the movie at any time. It can be played in sequence or out of sequence."

"So, let's add that to our diagram, Todd," said Dave. "**Simultaneous Activity** would be the first principle of a Short-Cycle Church Planting Team."

〰️

"Well, that is one tool in the tool belt. But there have to be more. What other principles besides simultaneous activity would enable a team of missionaries to plant a church faster?" asked Todd.

Ken began tapping his pencil on the table in a nervous fashion. He looked at the others like a poker player reluctant to play his chips. Dave refused to let him off the hook. "What'ya got, Ken?"

"I'm not sure I want to say."

"Why not?"

Ken turned his eyes upward and appeared to be very intent on the ceiling fan of the cabin. He was deep in thought. "This could be painful."

"Nothing could be more painful than being held hostage by the rebels in Tognumou. Come on. Cough it up."

"Okay, okay." Ken took a deep breath. Then he began, "Why do missionaries stay and stay and stay on a field? How come they are so slow to leave?"

Todd answered. "Because the church is not mature. Because there are still things for them to do."

"Wrong! We would like to believe that is the case, but it is not. The reason missionaries keep staying is because of a lack of trust. The reason missionaries never leave is because they don't trust the national believers to lead the church. And furthermore, they don't trust God and His Spirit to lead the national believers."

Ken continued. "I have been thinking about this for a long time. I have visited some of the fields in which our missionaries have been church planting for decades. In nearly every case, there are national leaders present that are

THERE IS NO TIME

more than capable of leading the church. Yet we continue to have a missionary presence there. My question is, Why? The answer I keep coming back to is, it's a lack of trust."

Ken looked over at Dave to gauge his response. But Dave's body posture did not reveal a defensiveness. Instead, it showed he was processing Ken's words. So, he continued on, "When I read through the book of Acts and when I study the Pauline epistles, I am amazed at the level of trust Paul exhibited. He left churches after a very brief period of time. Sometimes he was forced out. Often he just left and moved down the road to the next city. In either case, he had to display a high level of trust in the new believers and in God's ability to guide those believers through His Spirit and His Word."

Todd jumped in. "But isn't that risky?"

"Sure it is! Paul had no assurance the church would survive and thrive. But he also knew he had no assurance of that *even if* he stayed in the community. Every church will have problems! Believe me—as a pastor, I know that to be true. Every church will have problems because churches are filled with people. So, the objective is not to painstakingly perfect a church so that it will not fall into heresy. Instead, the objective is to rapidly raise up leaders and then exit—fully trusting God to guide them in leading His church."

Landis joined in, "Just last week, I read a compelling example of high trust in Paul's meeting with the Ephesian elders in Miletus in Acts 20. As he bids a final farewell to them, he also issues them a warning. He says, 'I know that after I leave, savage wolves will come in among you, and will not spare the flock. Even from your own number men will arise and distort the truth in order to draw away disciples after them.' In other words, Paul had revelation from God that showed this church would be attacked from without and from within. If we knew that, our natural response would have been to stay in the community and help guide the church through those difficult times. But Paul didn't do that. Instead, he says, 'Now I commit you to God and to the word of his grace, which can build you up and give you an inheritance.' In other words, even though Paul knew the challenges that were ahead for the church, he still chose to entrust them to God and to His Word. That's high trust!"

Dave listened to all this. Finally he spoke. "Guys, you are so right here. But I never realized it before. You naturally want to protect a new church from destructive influences— especially false doctrine. I am sure Paul, with his passion for truth, felt the same way. But ultimately that is impossible. And in seeking to do so, we are showing we don't trust the nationals to lead the church nor God's Spirit to guide them."

He paused for a moment. Then he said, "I admit it. I have been guilty of low trust."

"This is not a blame game, Dave," added Ken. "That's not the point. The point is that, if a Short-Cycle Church Planting team wants to establish a church faster, then they will have to exhibit high trust. For it is only with high trust that they will be able to step away with confidence, knowing their job is done."

"But is the job ever done?" asked Todd. "Do we just exit a field and never set foot in it again?"

"That is not what high trust means," replied Ken. "Paul returned to churches after he established them. He occasionally sent his co-workers like Timothy or Silas to check on a church. But that was in a role of encouragement and consultation. So, you can have high trust and still be a friend and counselor to a church. But you do so in an itinerant fashion, not as a local leader."

"Well, it looks like we need to add a second Short-Cycle principle to this diagram: **High Trust**," said Todd. "I like it. We're making progress."

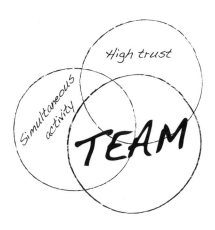

"I need a break," Dave said wearily. "How about if we take a hike through these beautiful mountains before supper?"

"I'm game!" shouted Todd as he jumped up from his chair. Waving a hand at the others he said, "Come on, you couch potatoes! Let's get some exercise and breathe some clean mountain air." They tumbled out the door with grunts of excitement and headed for the trails.

12

THREE MORE PRINCIPLES

The hike was helpful for clearing the head. After almost two hours on the trails and after another nice meal from the grill, the gang returned to their work refreshed and energetic.

"Okay—we have a high performance team at the center and two key principles identified: simultaneous activity and high trust," remarked Todd. "Let's try and finish up this work tonight if we can. What other Short-Cycle principles need to be identified?"

"Well, I have another one," said Dave. "It is one I am quite passionate about. I am not sure what to call it. Perhaps overt witness. But here is what I am talking about—I am talking about sowing the seed of the Gospel early, often and directly."

"But how is that different from traditional missions?" asked Todd. "Doesn't every missionary want to do that?"

"Well, yes and no. Every missionary wants to share the Gospel as soon as possible but most have been trained to practice relational evangelism. And in relational evangelism, you take time to build relationships with others—some call it 'earning the right to be heard'—with a view of one day crossing the bridge you have built with the truth of the Gospel."

"I know exactly what you are talking about," added Ken. "We have had evangelism seminars at our church that have preached much the same message."

"In North America and with church members living in their own culture, that probably is appropriate. But we have made the mistake of incorporating that into our church-planting strategy. It's a mistake for two reasons. First, it is a mistake because it takes time to build those relationships. And in a Short-Cycle philosophy, you do not have that luxury of time. Secondly, not only does it take time to build those relationships, but it can be unproductive time because you have no assurance that the people in whom you are investing time will ever become Christians. So, you could end up wasting considerable time in a series of relationships that bear no fruit."

Dave continued, "I had that very thing happen to me with the Fonu people. I took a considerable amount of time building a relationship with two sets of neighbors. In fact, they took a majority of my time. Eventually, I was able to share Christ with them. But they were such staunch Muslims they never came to faith. They respected me but they didn't believe my message. While I enjoyed their friendship, the time invested in them did nothing to advance the work of the church plant."

"So, how is an overt witness different from a relational approach?" asked Todd.

"Well, it is fundamentally different in its purpose.

While relational evangelism seeks to build relationship with a view to evangelism, an overt witness seeks to sow the seed as broadly and early as possible in order to identify those who respond to its message. While it seeks to be culturally appropriate, it does not shy away from being direct and even confrontational. Those who engage in relational evangelism seek to do so because they do not want to be offensive to their neighbors since they plan on living next to them for the rest of their lives. However, a Short-Cycle team does not plan on living in a country for a long period of time. They just want to find those God is in the process of drawing to Christ, build into them and then move on to the next location. We can have confidence God has people He desires to bring to Himself among every tribe, tongue and people because of the testimony of His Word. So, we seek to broadcast the seed as widely as we can, as early as we can, in an effort to pinpoint them."

Ken, with his theological mind spinning at full speed, responded, "If so, then that dramatically changes how we should view missionary evangelism. For the goal of a missionary is not to win a city or people group to Christ. Instead, the goal of a missionary is to find and win the two or three key people who will reach a community for Christ."

"That's right! Through overt witness you surface them. Then you build into them to equip others. Finally you turn them loose to infect their entire nation for the Gospel."

Todd interjected, "I get it! The missionaries are not there to reach a country for Christ. They are just there to plant the infection in the lives of a few who will spread it to everyone else."

"That makes sense, doesn't it?" asked Dave. "The best people for reaching a nation are not missionaries. The best people are the people themselves. An **Overt Witness** supports that."

"So, let's add that to our diagram," said Todd with approval.

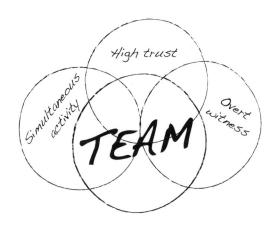

"Simultaneous activity. High trust. Overt witness. What other principles are necessary for a Short-Cycle team?"

Landis, who had been mostly silent during the previous discussion, spoke up. "I have something I have been thinking about. As you know, I am on the missions committee for our church. Because that is true, I have the opportunity to interview our missionaries and learn more about the nature of their ministries. I have to admit I often see a disturbing pattern."

"What's that?" asked Todd.

"Missionaries who create dependency by doing the work nationals could and should do."

"What do you mean?"

"I mean, well-intentioned missionaries who continue

to minister in various areas instead of allowing national believers to do so. Obviously, if it is a pure pioneering situation and there are no national believers, then it is necessary for the missionary to do everything. He or she has no choice. But once God brings people to faith, they can and must be involved in the ministry. And if we do anything for the national church that they can and should be doing, we are not helping them. We may think we are. But we are not. Instead, we are crippling them. And we are creating a dependency that is very difficult to eliminate later."

Dave spoke up. "Once again, I can confirm this from my own experiences on the field. No missionary wants to create dependency. We all want our churches to be self-supporting and self-governing. However, avoiding that is not as easy as it sounds. For nearly every day the missionary makes decisions that have the possibility of creating dependency in the church. So, avoiding dependency requires diligence and focus. If you lose that focus, you will inevitably end up doing things that encourage more dependency."

Landis added, "And it is a moving target. For as the church grows and matures, there is more they should be doing and less the missionary should be doing. In other words, you constantly have to be asking the question, What should I do in this situation?"

"How about this as a principle—We will do only what only we can do?" asked Ken. "This means we intentionally restrict the scope of our activity so we are doing things only the missionary can do. If the church can do it, they need to do it. But if not, we will do it because the work needs to be done. But we will do only what only we can do."

"I like it! But this really runs counter-intuitive for people," commented Dave. "And most missionaries are gracious,

THERE IS NO TIME

talented people who want to see the church succeed. So they
naturally are prone to be very involved in the church plant.
Therefore, this helps guide them to a strategic use of their
gifts so they minimize dependency in the church."

Todd raised a question. "What does this mean for
buildings and other projects like that? I agree wholeheartedly
with the principle here, but I think it also goes beyond just
the missionary involvement in ministry. For I see us creating
dependency also through Western funding of projects and
even financial support of national workers."

"Exactly!" said Dave. "I know of church groups from
North America who came and built enormous church
buildings in West Africa and really thought they were helping
the churches. In reality, they were creating an albatross
around their necks. For the church could never sustain or
maintain a building like that, so it became a huge financial
burden to them."

Ken asked, "But are we wrong not to share our resources
with brethren who have so little?"

"It depends on the kind of help we offer. If there is a
famine and people need food, then giving money or grain
does not create dependency. It saves lives and serves as a
testimony of the love of Christ. But if we seek to do something
for the church that they should do for themselves, such as
building a church building, then we run the risk of making
them dependent. It is the kind of help that hurts. So, we
have to constantly evaluate before we act so we 'do only what
only we can do.'"

Landis summed it up. "So we are talking about a Short-
Cycle principle that intentionally restricts the scope of
activity both in ministry and in projects so that we do not
create a dependency upon the missionary, the mission or

Western funding sources."

"What do we call it?" asked Todd.

"How about **Restricted Scope**?" said Dave. "Like Landis said, we restrict the scope of our activities so we don't create dependency in the church."

The gang seemed agreeable to the title, so Todd added it to the diagram.

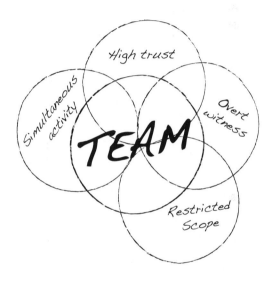

"Well, that looks like a nice assortment of tools for the Short-Cycle team to use as they seek to plant churches faster," said Todd. "Are we finished?"

"Not yet," replied Landis. "I still have one more idea. And hear me out on this. We want the Short-Cycle team to plant churches in as short a time as possible, correct?"

Everyone mumbled their affirmative answer to his question.

Landis continued. "Well, if so, then the team will have

to become experts at spotting leverage."

"Leverage?" queried Dave.

"Yes, leverage," answered Landis. "Leverage is what allows work to be completed at an accelerated pace. For instance, think of the levers you use in your daily life. A pulley is a tool that gives leverage. It allows you to multiply your strength and lift a heavy object easier. The same thing is true for a car jack. Well, in a similar way, if a team wants to accelerate their efforts in church planting, they need to become skilled at identifying and using leverage."

Dave had a confused look on his face. "Landis, you are losing me now. Put this in clearer terms for me. How does leverage relate to a team of missionaries doing church planting?"

"Look at it this way—if I have a task to complete, and I want to accomplish it faster, I look for something that will give me tactical advantage. I look for something that will multiply my efforts."

"Such as…?"

"Let's say you have a team going to a Muslim country in East Africa. And let's say they discover through careful observation something they would not have expected in the culture—like a fascination with Old Western movies."

"How could anyone be fascinated with Old Westerns?" deadpanned Todd, no fan of anything starring horses or cowboy hats.

Landis ignored him and continued. "If so, they could possibly leverage that for their work by hosting Old West movie nights and using that for spreading the seed of the Gospel. Or, let's say they find a secret believer in a high-level position in the provincial government. If so, they could then leverage that relationship to avoid unwanted harassment from the police."

"I think I get it," said Dave.

"Let me give you another example: let's say just before you enter a new country with a Short-Cycle team, there is major political upheaval causing general unrest throughout the country."

"That doesn't sound inviting to me," commented Ken.

"But it can be if you look at it strategically," answered Landis. "For whenever there is upheaval of the status quo, there is also opportunity for societal change. That gives a welcome window for the Gospel. All of this is leverage. All of this is tactical advantage. Assuming you have strategic thinkers on every team, you can train the team to look for and seize tactical advantage when it presents itself."

"Do you look for it only in the early stages when you are seeking to spread the gospel as widely as possible?" asked Dave.

"No—you look for it in everything you are doing. It doesn't matter if you are evangelizing, discipling or leading, you would always be seeking something that would further accelerate your work so it can be done faster. Sometimes it would be a person. Sometimes it would be a cultural insight. Sometimes it would be a piece of technology. But you are always trying to seize that tactical advantage."

Todd jumped in. "We did this during football games. I remember a time when the opposing team lost its best cornerback to a knee injury in the second quarter. Our coaches saw his replacement was an untested backup and immediately called several plays designed to seize the new advantage. We overwhelmed this new guy and easily won the game."

"I think we attempt to use leverage in our ministry at

times," said Dave.

"I am sure you do," answered Landis. "Especially if you have a strategic mind. But this principle would mean the whole team would be very intentional and purposeful about identifying and seizing **Tactical Advantage**."

"Okay, let's add it to our diagram," added Todd. "This gives us five principles for the Short-Cycle team— Simultaneous Activity, High Trust, Overt Witness, Restricted Scope, and Tactical Advantage."

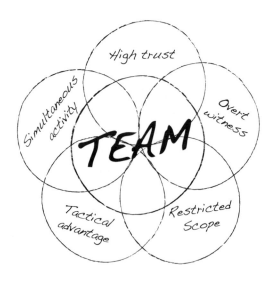

"Hey guys, do you see what I see?" asked Ken.

"What?" answered Todd.

"Look at the first letter of each of those five principles. Look at the acronym it spells—SHORT! Simultaneous activity. High trust. Overt witness. Restricted scope. Tactical advantage. It spells SHORT. That is a perfect way to remember the five principles for Short-Cycle teams."

"Perhaps this is another example of divine serendipity!" laughed Dave.

"It may be," added Landis. "But the real test will be whether this works on the field." He paused. "I think our job is done, guys."

"I agree," said Dave. "We came here to discover a new model for church planting. Each of you brought valuable expertise to the table. The synergy present produced a truly innovative approach. It represents a rare combination of insight from missionaries, pastors, corporate execs and business people. It far exceeds what I thought might happen. I don't know how to thank you...."

"We didn't come here for accolades, Dave," interrupted Todd. "We are just as interested in reaching this world for Christ as you are. You have the privilege of being on the front lines. We don't. But as part of the global supply chain, we are passionate about seeing new churches started in the unreached parts of this world."

"And if this input helps move missions forward, then it has been a good investment of our time and energy," added Landis. The others nodded their heads in agreement.

Tomorrow they would all head in different directions. Dave knew his ministry as a church planter could not and should not ever be the same. The starting place now would be a team—a real team. The team would utilize Short-Cycle principles in their work. And they would believe God to do a God-sized work through them.

Dave could hardly wait to start!

13

BACK ON THE FIELD

Three years have passed since the gang gathered in Colorado. While not easy, Dave succeeded in persuading the home office of All-World Missions to try a Short-Cycle Church Planting team. Three couples and two singles, all redeployed from other fields, joined Dave in two weeks of intensive team training, led by both corporate team trainers and mission strategists.

After considerable research, the team decided to go to the capital of a Central Asian country which had well less than 1 percent evangelicals. Each member of the team had a specific role, based on giftedness and strengths. Dave was the evangelist of the group. He was grateful others were gifted in strategic thinking and administration.

The language was difficult to learn and the culture proved challenging. But utilizing the disaster-relief platform developed by another Christian agency, the team began to put Short-Cycle principles into operation. Aware of the volatility of the region, they established a five-year timeline for the work. The goal was certainly aggressive—to plant two reproducing churches. They knew this was a God-sized challenge in this historically resistant land. But they kept returning to the main elements of their faith context: the Power of the Gospel, Divine Serendipity, God's Ability and the Primacy of Prayer.

Using the principle of Overt Witness, the team was able to see two influential people in the community come to faith in Christ in the first year. Leaders were developed in a simultaneous fashion with other strategic initiatives. As the number of national believers slowly grew and as the people matured in their faith, the team showed more and more restraint in their personal ministries. No buildings were built or even considered. When problems developed in the church, missionaries consulted with the church but showed trust in the leadership to discover biblical solutions. A second plant began to emerge from the first.

The process was not complete yet. More training and maturity was still needed. But Dave already saw the end in sight. In less than two years, the bulk of the work would be complete and the team would disengage, save some on-going consultation.

And then…? Dave already knew the answer.

He was already dreaming of his second Short-Cycle team to another part of the world.

After this I looked and there before me was a great multitude that no one could count, from every nation, tribe, people and language, standing before the throne and in front of the Lamb. They were wearing white robes and were holding palm branches in their hands. And they cried out in a loud voice: "Salvation belongs to our God, who sits on the throne, and to the Lamb."

REVELATION 7:9-10

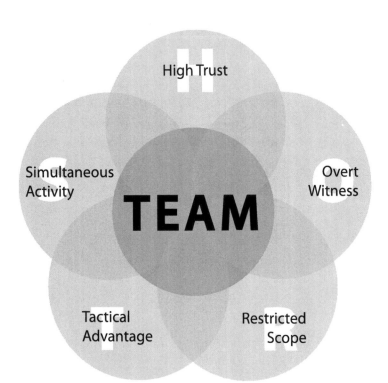

Short-Cycle Church Planting Model

ABOUT AVANT MINISTRIES

Avant Ministries is an interdenominational faith mission that has been sending church-planting missionaries to the most unreached parts of the world since 1892. Based in Kansas City and governed by an International Board of Directors, Avant today has over 300 missionaries serving in over twenty countries seeking to establish mature, reproducing churches where the church does not exist.

For more information, contact Avant at:

Avant Ministries	**Avant Ministries Canada**
10000 North Oak Trafficway	2121 Henderson Highway
Kansas City, MO 64155	Winnipeg, MB R2G 1P8
816.734.8500	204.338.7831
fax 816.734.4601	fax 204.339.3321
info@avmi.org	AMC@avmi.org

www.AvantMinistries.org